Perry the Purple Pup

Kathy Tschida

Trilogy Christian Publishers
A Wholly Owned Subsidiary of Trinity Broadcasting Network
2442 Michelle Drive
Tustin, CA 92780

Copyright © 2020 by Kathy Tschida

All Scripture quotations, unless otherwise noted, taken from THE HOLY BIBLE, NEW INTERNATIONAL VERSION®, NIV® Copyright © 1973, 1978, 1984, 2011 by Biblica, Inc.® Used by permission. All rights reserved worldwide.

Scripture quotations marked (KJV) taken from *The Holy Bible, King James Version*. Cambridge Edition: 1769.

All rights reserved, including the right to reproduce this book or portions thereof in any form whatsoever.

For information, address Trilogy Christian Publishing
Rights Department, 2442 Michelle Drive, Tustin, Ca 92780.
Trilogy Christian Publishing/ TBN and colophon are trademarks of Trinity Broadcasting Network.

For information about special discounts for bulk purchases, please contact Trilogy Christian Publishing.

Manufactured in the United States of America

Trilogy Disclaimer: The views and content expressed in this book are those of the author and may not necessarily reflect the views and doctrine of Trilogy Christian Publishing or the Trinity Broadcasting Network.

10 9 8 7 6 5 4 3 2 1

Library of Congress Cataloging-in-Publication Data is available.

ISBN 978-1-64773-726-9 (Print Book)
ISBN 978-1-64773-727-6 (ebook)

Dedication

To my Savior Jesus and my husband Paul, both who love me unconditionally. And to my dad, who instilled in me a love for Jesus, reading, and music.

Acknowledgments

Thank you to my husband, Paul, my daughter, and the rest of my family and friends who have encouraged and helped me along this journey. Thank you to Jesus who gave me this story and the courage to share it with you. Thank you also to the great staff at TBN and Trilogy Publishing for believing in me and my story.

Perry the purple pup is a special dog. He has a secret.

One day, Perry goes to the park and meets Sam the sad Siberian. Sam is hurt because he broke his paw and cannot play in the park today. Sam has to sit and watch the other dogs play.

Perry asks Sam, "Can I help you?" Sam says, "No, no one can help me. My paw is broken."

Perry tries again. "I would like to help you. Do you want me to stay here with you? I do have a way I can help."

Sam again says, "No." Sam does not want Perry's help. Sam had prayed for healing, not for help from a purple pup. Too bad Sam does not know Perry's secret.

The next day, Perry the purple pup goes back to the park and meets Goldie the grumpy Golden. Goldie is grumpy because her owners moved and left her behind.

Perry happily asks, "Can I help you?" Goldie says in a grumpy voice, "No," and she turns away from Perry.

Perry tries again, not giving up.
"Can I help make you happy?"

Goldie, again in her grumpy voice, says, "No, I do not want help from a purple pup." Goldie had prayed for her owners to come back, not for help from a purple pup. Too bad Goldie does not know Perry's secret.

The next day, Perry goes back to the park and meets Larry the lonely Lab. Larry is lonely because he does not have any friends. Perry gladly asks, "Can I help you?"

Larry looks at Perry with his lonely eyes and says, "How could you help me?" Perry says, "I will help if you want me to."

Larry had prayed for a friend, but he doesn't want a friend who is purple. Other dogs might think he is weird. So, Larry says, "No, thanks. I'll be okay." Too bad Larry does not know Perry's secret either.

One last time, Perry goes back to the park. He meets Beast the bully Bulldog. Beast is the bully of the park, but Perry does not care. Perry asks with a smile, "Can I help you?"

Beast is surprised that any dog would talk to him without being scared. Beast does not answer because Beast hopes Perry will go away. But no one knows Beast has prayed for God to help him change.

Perry asks again, "Can I help you?" Beast quietly says, "Yes. I know I'm a bully. But I want to change. Can you help me change so I can have friends?"

Perry says, "Yes, I can help you. I have a secret. I am an angel who has been trying to help answer prayers all week. I would love to give you the answer to your prayers." Beast is silent, not sure what to say. So, he nods his head slowly.

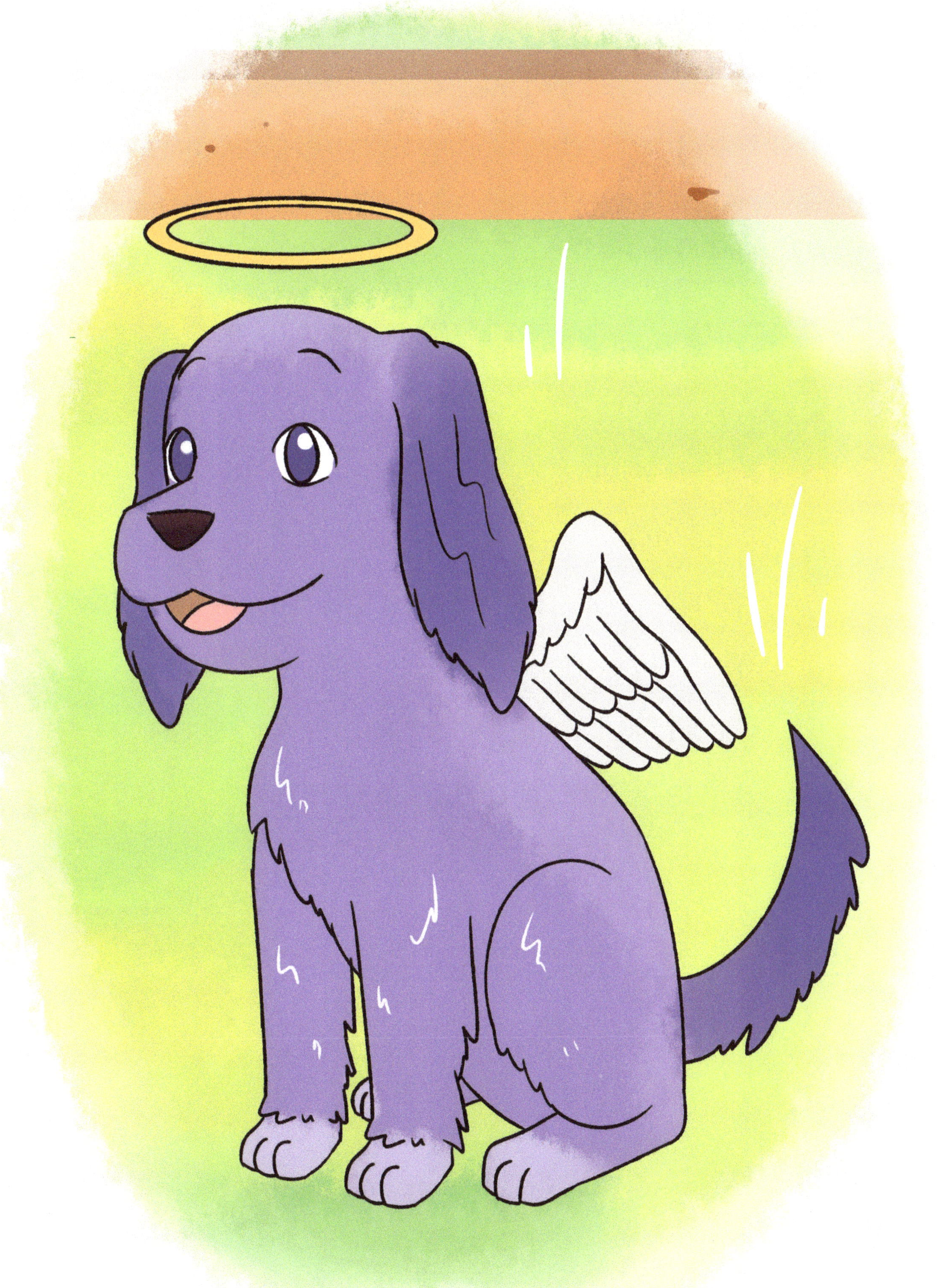

Perry says, "God wants to answer prayers. I am glad you let me help you. God will change your heart. He will show you how to be a friend so you can have friends."

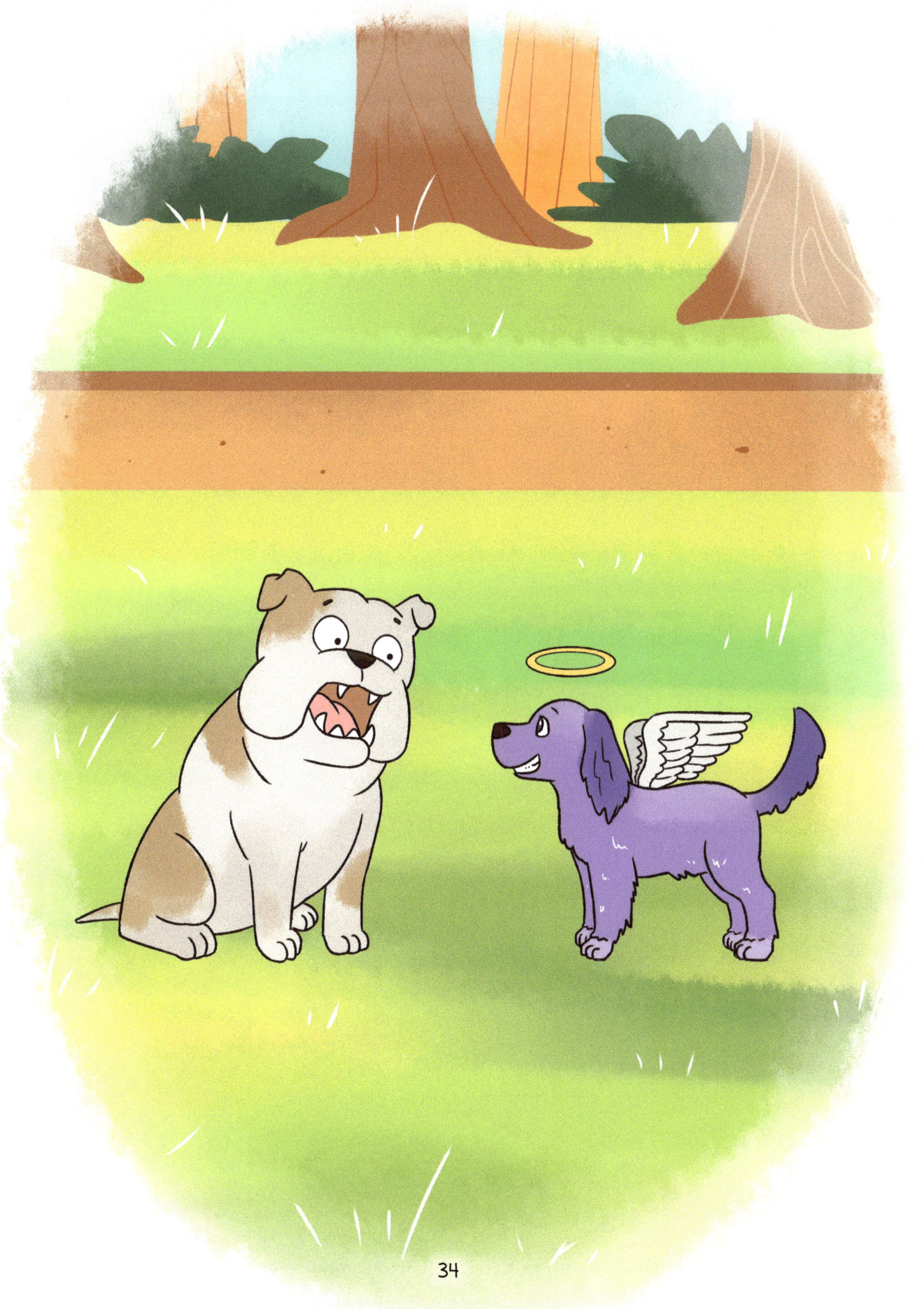

Beast nods again, glad he let this odd purple pup help him.

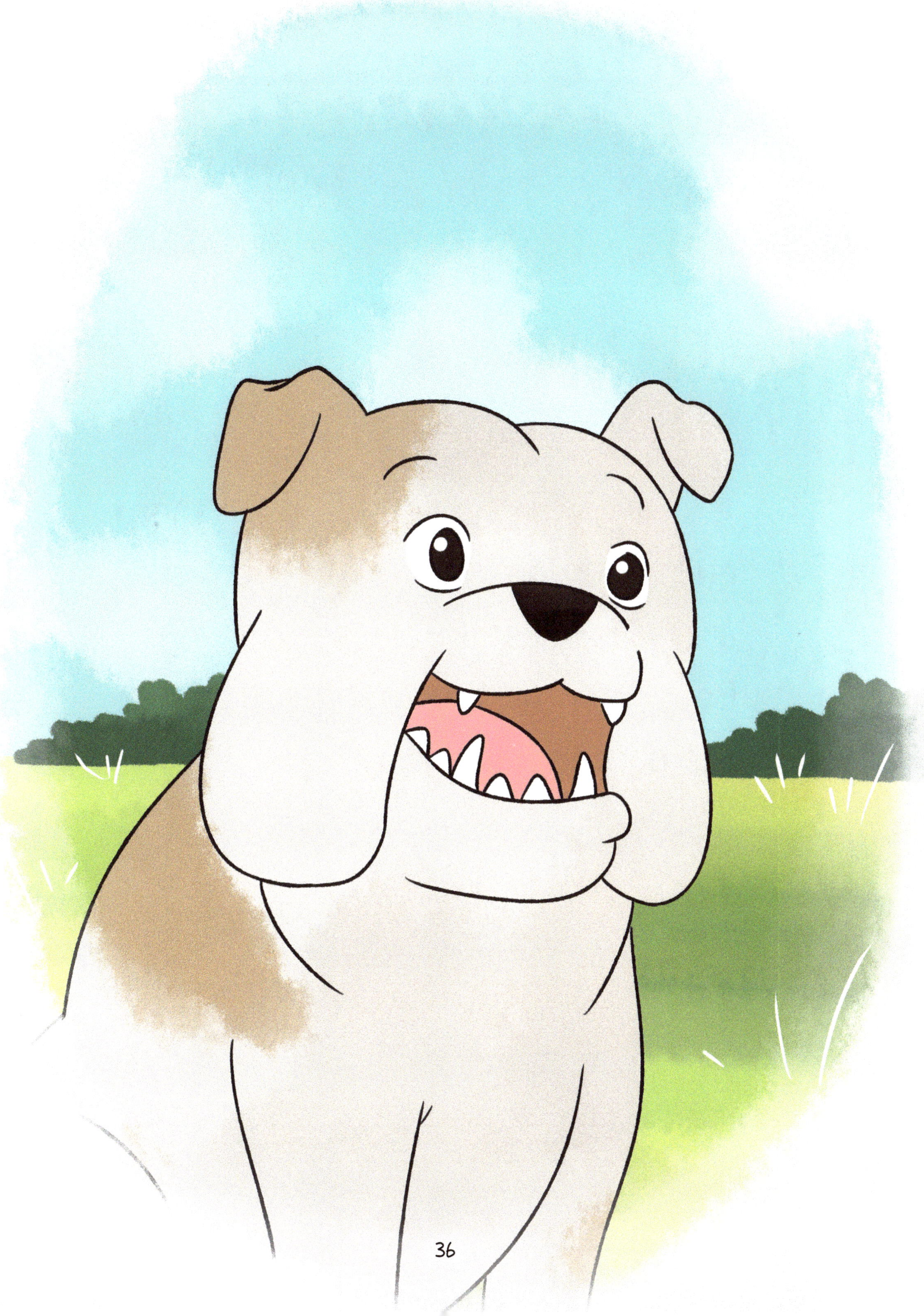

Two months later, Perry the purple pup looks down from heaven and sees Beast the blessed Bulldog. Beast is now the favorite dog in the park to play with.

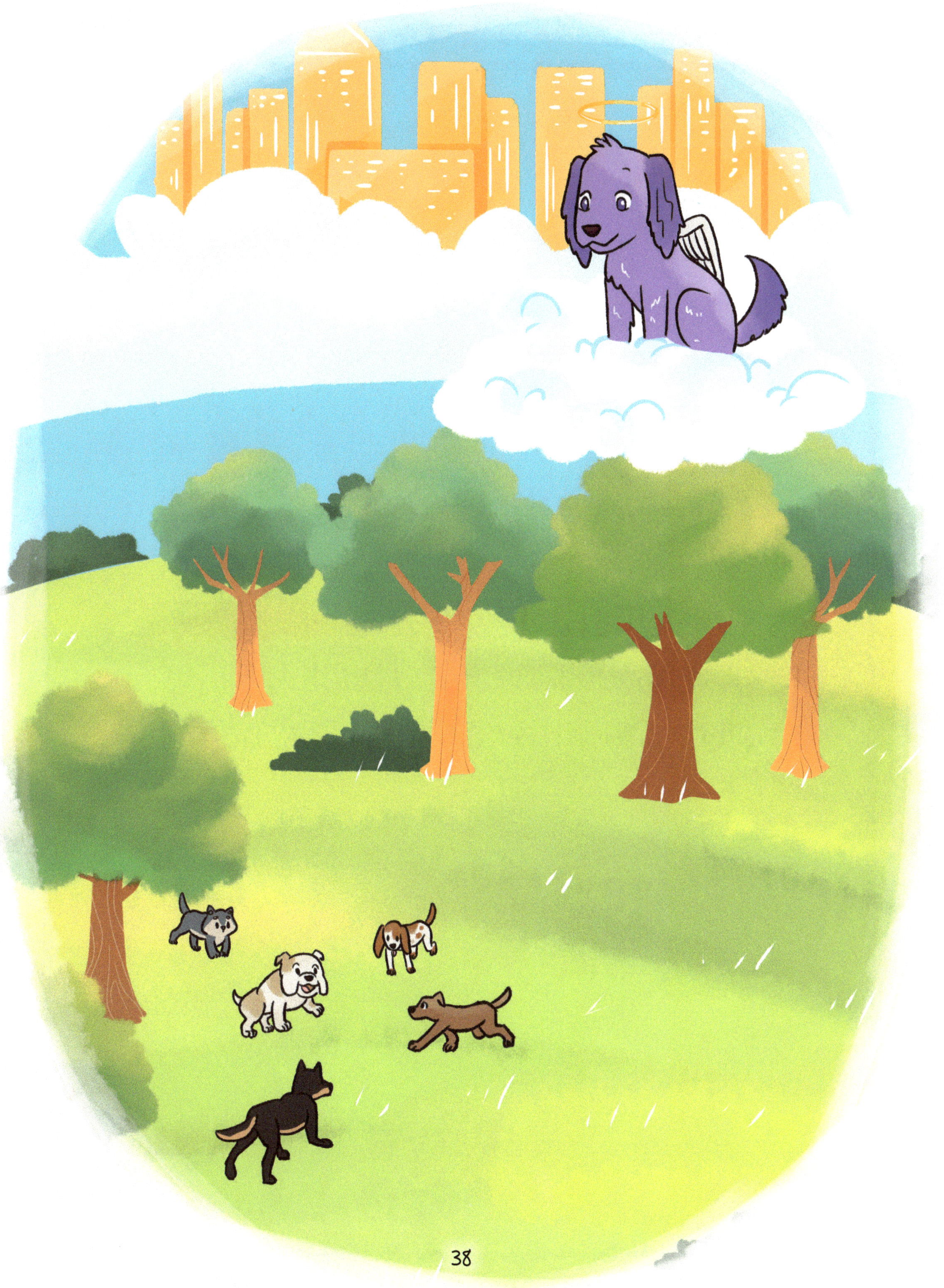

Beast stops by a tree and says, "Thank you, God, for sending your angel, Perry the purple pup. Thank you for helping me. Thank you for all my new friends. In Jesus' name, amen."

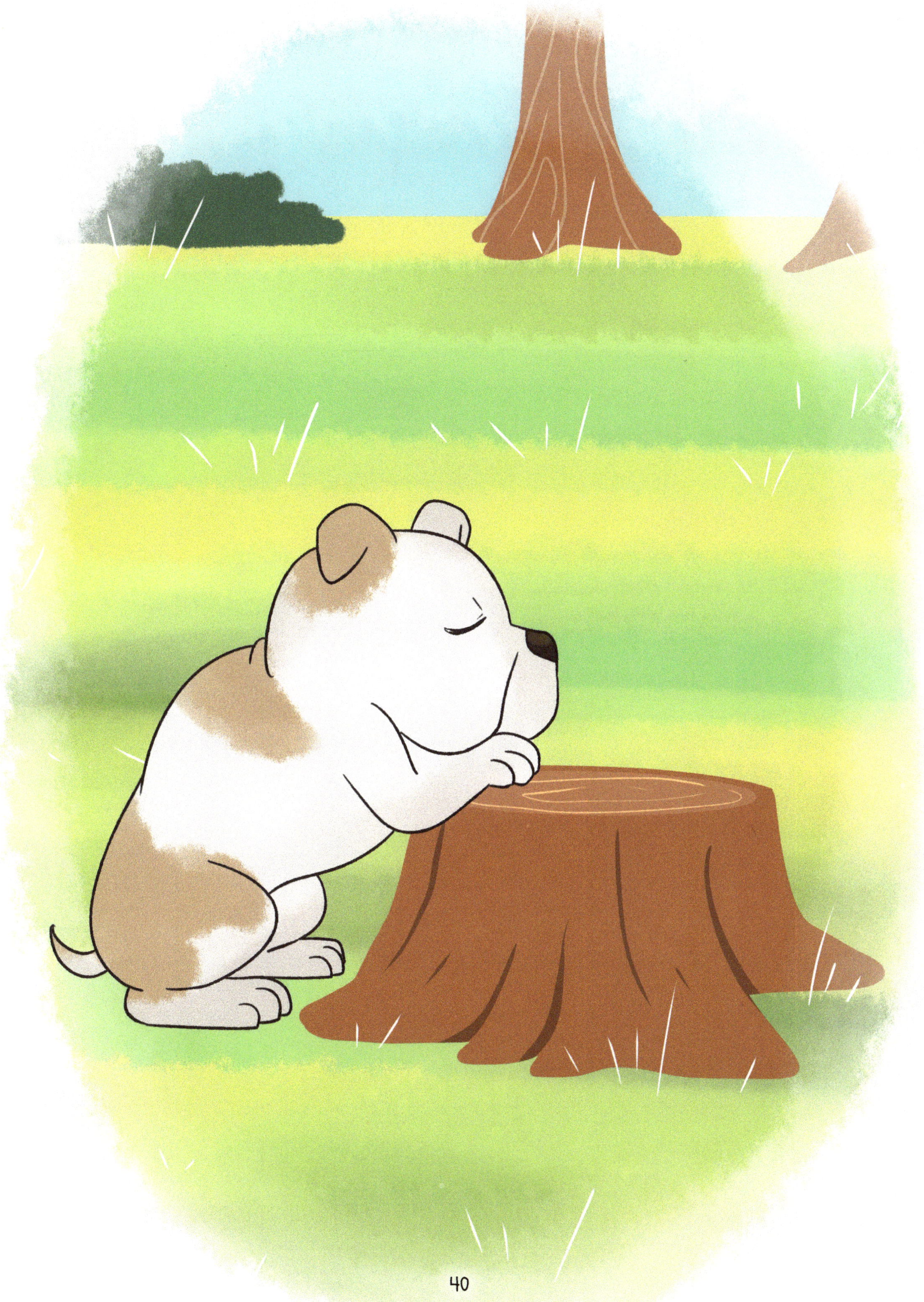

Discussion questions

- What do you think Perry wanted to do for Sam the sad Siberian?
- What do you think Perry wanted to do for Goldie the grumpy Golden?
- What do you think Perry wanted to do for Larry the lonely Lab?
- Why was God's help turned down by Sam, Goldie, and Larry? (See Heb 13:2, John 13:20 and John 1:10-11)
- How did Beast change because he let God help him? (see Proverbs 18:24a)
- How can you be more friendly?
- Does God always answer your prayers how you thought He should? Tell about a time He answered your prayers in a way you did not expect.
- What does Psalm 91:15 mean to you?
- Do you know Jesus? If not, you can. Pray this, "Dear Jesus, I know I do wrong things, and I need you to forgive me. I believe You died so I can be forgiven of all the wrong I do. I believe You came back to life after three days. Come into my life. I want You to be my Savior and Friend. Amen." (See Romans 10:9)

- Hebrews 13:2 Don't forget to show hospitality to strangers, for some who have done this have entertained angels without realizing it!
- John 13:20 I tell you the truth, anyone who welcomes my messenger is welcoming me, and anyone who welcomes me is welcoming the Father who sent me.
- John 1:10-11 He came into the very world he created, but the world didn't recognize him. He came to his own people, and even they rejected him.
- Proverbs 18:24a (NKJV) A man who has friends must himself be friendly.
- Psalm 91:15 When they call on me, I will answer; I will be with them in trouble. I will rescue and honor them.
- Romans 10:9 If you openly declare that Jesus is Lord and believe in your heart that God raised him from the dead, you will be saved.

About the Author

Kathy Tschida is a former elementary music teacher who has loved reading her whole life. As a child, she would often fall asleep while reading a good book and always loved having her dad read to her. She is passionate about her Savior and wants all to know that God is the best, most loving Father. Kathy is married, she has a daughter, and she has a Miniature Schnauzer. She is also a singer, composer, and pianist who loves worshipping with believers of all ages.

www.kathytschida.com

CPSIA information can be obtained
at www.ICGtesting.com
Printed in the USA
BVHW020924070121
597226BV00003B/10

9 781647 737269